Winter Music

SARAH KIRSCH

Winter Music

SELECTED POEMS
translated by
MARGITT LEHBERT

Anvil Press Poetry

Published in 1994
by Anvil Press Poetry Ltd
69 King George Street London SE10 8PX

Copyright © Sarah Kirsch 1994
Translations and preface copyright © Margitt Lehbert 1994

This book is published
with financial assistance from
The Arts Council

Designed and composed by Anvil
Photoset in Melior by Typestream
Printed and bound in England
by The Arc & Throstle Press, Todmorden, Lancs

ISBN 0 85646 234 9

ACKNOWLEDGEMENTS

The poems in this selection are published by kind
permission of Sarah Kirsch's German publishers. For
poems from *Landaufenthalt* (1977), *Zaubersprüche* (1974),
Rückenwind (1977) and *Drachensteigen* (1979), we thank
Langewiesche-Brandt KG Verlag, Ebenhausen bei
München; for poems from *Erdreich* (1982), *Katzenleben*
(1984) and *Schneewärme* (1989), Deutsche Verlags-Anstalt
GmbH, Stuttgart.

Where two publication dates are listed in the Contents, the
first is that of publication in the former GDR.

This translation has been made possible in part by a grant
from the Wheatland Foundation, New York.

Contents

6   *Contents*

From TAIL WIND (*Rückenwind*, 1976, 1977)

From KITE FLYING (*Drachensteigen*, 1979)

Preface

TIELENHEMME is a village so small you will hunt for it in vain in your atlas. It is accessible neither by rail nor by inter-city bus; you can hitch a ride on the local school bus, if school happens to be in session, but otherwise you need a car, a detailed map and a willingness to stop and ask for directions when you get lost. It is this seclusion, this northern landscape that Sarah Kirsch has celebrated in her recent books of poetry. The light here is often grey, with low-hanging clouds skating in from the North Sea over the flat, sparsely populated stretch of land that lies immediately south of Denmark. A different Germany, this, a Germany not shaped by crowds, industry or speed. Tidal basins and fens mark the landscape, and in winter the occasional bare tree stands out in sharp relief against thin accumulations of snow.

The houses of the village huddle up against the dikes of the Eider river. The fertile loam of the regions farther south has given way here to marshy soil with a thin layer of marl near the river; drainage ditches frame the fields, keeping the earth barely dry enough to grow a few hesitant crops. For miles around you see no houses; the soil is too damp, too prone to shifting, for any buildings to be erected. Against this barren landscape, where Sarah Kirsch lives in an old converted school house, caring for her garden and her animals, the angels and speaking crows of her poetry become imaginable, almost tangible, as though the magic of the surroundings had swept away all scepticism with its stark beauty.

Sarah Kirsch was born in Limlingerode, a tiny town in the Harz mountains, on April 16, 1935. Her given name was Ingrid Bernstein; she changed her first name in protest against Germany's history and her father's anti-Semitism, and her last name during a brief marriage. After completing her Abitur, the German equivalent to A-levels, she went to work in a sugar factory and later moved to Halle to study biology. Her mother had taken her on long walks as a child, teaching her the names of plants and animals they saw and kindling an interest that carried her through a degree in biology and a love of nature that is apparent in her poetry. She wrote her thesis on the ectoparasites of mice – their lice, fleas and mites – and to research it she spent a year setting up mouse-traps in and around Halle, rising early every day to collect her catch. She would use the same exact and detached attention to detail in her poetry, showing her ability to focus on the plain, normally disregarded aspects of life.

While working on her degree, she met a number of young writers. Despite her complete ignorance of poetry – or because of it, as she jokes today – she joined a literary circle led by Gerhard Wolf and began to write. From 1963 to 1965, the authorities let her attend the prestigious Johannes-R.-Becher Institute for Literature in Halle, where she studied under Georg Maurer. Wolf and Maurer were to influence an entire generation of East German poets. With their emphasis on writing about those things with which one is intimately acquainted, they taught young poets to write what has become known as the 'poetry of the small object'. And a strong visual image is at the centre of most poems by Sarah Kirsch, the image of something familiar:

> The cuckoo stutters and the baked beds
> Tear apart when I haul my watering cans
> Look helplessly at the plants placed in my care
> Lice-ridden vegetables, . . .

But the invisible, the magical, the mythological turn up right alongside her description of everyday objects, mentioned without a change in tone or language, calmly accepted as fact. It is as though her angels were as much a part of the natural order as trees or gardens, as though a casual reference to the black soul of crows were not calculated to surprise. The creatures in her poetry live on the edge between magic and the quotidian, and precisely because of their magic, they illumine the quotidian sharply:

> . . . a scattered angel
> Appears before me to rescue
> Twenty-seven rose trees the yellow canister

Strapped over his mildewed wings
His heavenly thumb in a rubber glove
Lowers the valve and for hours
There's the smell of bitter almonds.

Throughout her work, her love for nature and its painstaking description is clouded by the knowledge of its progressive destruction. Where she creates an idyll, saws, bulldozers, chemicals are sure to intrude, showing how precarious it is. No garden, however enchanted, is safe any more.

After she had been admitted to the East German Writers' Union in the early Sixties, Sarah Kirsch was sent to an agricultural collective and to an industrial plant so she could 'learn' to write socialist realism. But most of her poetry remained centred on love and nature. Politics rarely found its way into her work, and much frustrated criticism was written about her on both sides of the inner-Germany border in the Sixties and Seventies, with people reading political subjects that she had never intended into her poetry. By the late Sixties, she was caught in the crossfire of official East German cultural politics. For one thing, her work was considered too melancholy to illustrate the proper reaction to the new socialist reality, and it contained little that officials could construe as desirable political commitment. Her poem 'Black Beans' was sharply attacked at the Sixth Writers' Congress in 1969. Interestingly enough, thanks to a cultural thaw that had begun two years earlier, the same poem would be cited in 1973 to illustrate the diversity of East German literature.

In 1977, a series of events occurred that were to change Kirsch's life. During that year, she added her signature to a public letter asking the government to reconsider its *de facto* exiling of Wolf Biermann, a popular writer of political songs and a vocal critic of the East German régime. While on an officially sanctioned trip to the West, he had given a controversial and now famous performance in Cologne. Soon after this concert, he discovered that he had been stripped of his East German citizenship and would not be permitted to return home. This development angered and alarmed writers and artists in the East because it signalled the danger of even tighter control over their work. Their public letter and the government's reaction to it changed the literary and artistic scene in the GDR and caused many writers to emigrate to the West.

Signing it had decisive consequences for Kirsch's professional life. She was barred from both the Writers' Union and the Party, which meant her work was unlikely to be published again. There were repercussions in her personal life, too. After her divorce in 1968, she had moved to East Berlin; now a notice on the bulletin board of her apartment building informed her and other tenants that it would be best for all concerned if she moved. It was in this unnerving atmosphere that she, like many others, decided to leave; she applied for an official permission to emigrate – which was quickly granted – and moved from East to West Berlin on August 28, 1977. The first poem she wrote in West Berlin, 'Kite Flying', ends with the line: 'The rest of the string is ours, and that we knew you.' After that, she resolutely faced her new world, and much of her poetry focused on her travels.

She spent a few years in West Berlin, but took time off for the trips she had longed to take when she still lived in the East. In 1981, she left West Berlin to move to a small village near Bremen before buying her house in Tielenhemme.

Sarah Kirsch had been used by the GDR to show the diversity of its poetry. She would add diversity to any country's literature. Gliding enjambements and the frequent omission of punctuation send the reader back over sections of her poems in search of syntactical meaning; they offer resistance to any quick, superficial reading. In fact some of her lines never yield a 'correct' reading but remain ambiguous, coaxing the reader to produce a new version each time the poem is read. The English translation has not attempted to normalize the text or its punctuation. I hope that by doing this, I have created versions that in their turn send the reader back to puzzle the texts out in a meditative, enjoyable way.

MARGITT LEHBERT
Berlin, January 1992

Winter Music

By the White Pansies

By the white pansies
In the park like he told me to
I stand beneath the willow
Uncombed old woman leafless
You see she says he's not coming

Oh I say he's broken his foot
Swallowed a fish bone, a street
Was suddenly relocated or
He can't escape from his wife
Many things hinder us humans

The willow sways and creaks
Could also be he's dead already
Looked pale when he kissed you under your coat
Could be willow could be
So let's hope he doesn't love me any more

Journey I

The soil in our parts is in a bad way
Winter went like war its rags
Filthy dressings are decaying, scars
And scurf are welling forth, the earth
In our parts is scabby

Felted pale grass, pubic hair
Stretches over the biggest holes, the earth
In clayey gentle bloody groans beneath the dry sky

The transparent trees are so easily injured
That they stand totally still models of glass

Only the sword-flags in the linesman's yard
Beat their way unswervingly out of the earth
The tips of their leaves are tearing
For the first it's the worst

When He Has to Go to War

I swing myself into the apple tree
Tie myself fast with my hair
I shall wait for you Golden One
One month or more in the wind

Oh how the wind grips then
How the rain rattles the tree
The sun already sawing at my dress
Oh when my beloved approaches in his cloud of flame
I'll stand naked

For the birds bread and a house
For the birds that don't exist
I go pregnant with nightingales beloved
Wait for you come look at me

One Day

One day I shall be unscrupulously happy, then
The news will reach me, I don't know
If it's summer if it's watery snow, could be
I'm peeling potatoes (attempting a strip
Without lifting the knife)

Someone will find out before me, he tells me over
The phone, possibly I won't answer
Replace the receiver, smoke a cigarette
Turn on the radio, water my plants
Or I'll go out on the street into stores onto squares
To notice that everything goes on as usual
People press forward, somewhere else
A rally is being organized, microphone-check
The speaker writes a boring speech

On this day
I'll love marching music and shawms
I'll be waiting for him when the news reaches me
The war is over, those I don't call my brothers, fall
A swarm of flies, with their planes, ships, cannons
Back into their country

Legend of Lilya

1

No one knows if she was beautiful especially since
The testimony of surviving camp inmates
Is inconsistent even the colour of her hair
Is variously described in the files
There was no picture it was said
She'd been sent from Poland

2

In summer Lilya went barefoot as in winter and wrote
Seven letters

3

Six wire-thin little rolls wander
Through prisoners' overalls across the roll-call square cling
To tired skin disturb sleep reach
Someone who remains unknown (he can't bear
Witness at the trial)

4

The seventh someone gave for bread

5

Lilya in the orderly-room Lilya on her way Lilya in the
    shelter
Lash of the whip the name why won't she say anything who
    knows

Why is she silent in August when birds
Are singing in the smoke

6

One man in uniform skull insignia on his collar lover
Of old theatre pieces (his dog with a classical name)
    devised
They should let her eyes talk for her

7

Through the captured men they made a street
A strange avenue of plundered trees opened up
Here she was to walk and betray one of them

8

Now use your eyes Lilya order
The muscles the blood to be carefree here you've walked
    often
You know every stone every
Stone

9

Her face went by
Said the survivors they
Trembled Lilya as if dead walked walked
Until the man whose dog's name was Hamlet
Roared ordered enough

10

After that she was never seen again

11

Other witnesses say she smiled at everyone
On her way combed her hair with her fingers
Went straight to the gas (that was
More than twenty years ago)

12

They all spoke of Lilya for a long time

13

In the year '65 the judges in Frankfurt put on record
Obviously
Legends were being told this point
Should be struck from the list of charges

14

It's rumoured the letter said we
Won't get out of here we've
Seen too much

The Birds Sing Most Beautifully in the Rain

Even before day breaks rain falls the clouds rage lose them-
selves know no bounds water pearls earthward onto the
tips of trees flows along the keels of poplars moves from
needle to needle throws itself into the grass presses it down
jumps fragile veronicas drums the horizon out of the world

Brown diving ducks run over the water leave the reeds are
completely surrounded by water their feathers are ready for
the fat rain they dive to the bottom of the lake disclose to
the eels the earth floats

It rains into the nests of the little birds in trees and bushes
in the grass if they duck will they survive the flood they
just sing and call louder than the drops make sounds I
already distinguish cuckoo thrush quite a few doves
warblers join in and the sparrows over the window offer
their little bit the noise is great and full of art

Someone Is Getting Coals

Someone is getting coals
They clatter into the cellar
All the pigeons are on the roof one
Has breasts and looks out over the city
The rain clatters onto the coals before they're in the cellar
The pigeon in the rain is on the look-out for a
Wonderful event

It could be a car
That cuts the corners, out gets the grey-eyed driver
He sweats precious stones into his fiery beard so quickly
Did he drive he has a beautiful mouth half-long hair
Puts on a padded suit rubber boots
Because the weather's bad he's stacking briquettes
Everyone sees him as I described him he stands
In their heads
I've talked them into it

My Well-Travelled Friends Report to Me

My well-travelled friends report to me
How things are in the world, speak at my table
Of various countries, for example Italy
In front of the Doge's Palace innumerable pigeons walk
Form themselves
Into patterns, barely fly up, have
Their eye on the pavement the cracks with
Edibles: on the twelfth of June a cat came, its tail
Lay close to the ground, it
Came closer in a spiral, stalked
The eating birds, people
Gathered, began placing bets on the spectacle's outcome
But
A man crossed the square who saw nothing, all the birds
Clouded the old palace, the spectators swore,
In one country
A peasant woman rode over a glacier to
Save time in a pressing matter
Reached the city got off her horse
And didn't know why she'd come, had lost
Her mind in the ice, others again
Visited Lily Brik whose husband
Builds radios as a hobby
They say she's still lovely, wears
The oval ring Mayakovsky
Gave her on a long chain, one speaks
Of a village on the Mediterranean, the inhabitants
Are poor the older ones were all
Without exception partisans, now they catch fish
Fry them with their few guests sing songs
They pour out grain
For a half-blind mule

That carried weapons through the mountains, only
From the narrow country
Whose jungles and fields are being defoliated, where
Bombs are bursting there are heroes and graves, there
Is no news, none
Of my friends are there yet

Sinaia

They liked that, a castle in the mountains
High as a mountain and still more towers and battlements
And copper flags there were many to receive
One hall opens the next, weapons
Of all countries united
Knights threaten from empty bellies (horses
What did they have to carry) now columns
Ten metres high precious carvings
Alabaster gold busts mirrors
Manufactured in Venice, there are stacks of it
They came from Germany and loved
The hunt in particular (only a few books) I
On their exquisite floors in the Turkish room
In the huge hall, before I'd come through villages
Now understood the revolutions
I naked in this lair of thieves became willing
To smash it, even the sad mirrors
Wine onto the carpets down with everything where
Are my comrades a match open doors the wind
Finishes the job, who says
Any object here
Was worth saving I say it later

Return

My friend lives in the country there
One flock of sheep moves past the window twice a day
Once in the evening another, the house is friendly
The husband wise kind almost beautiful the
Children healthy everything fine, in the morning
My friend sings when she bathes the baby
Gives away apples to everyone, the sun
Looks very beautiful in the weeping willows
Dahlias have unfolded their leaves dust settles softly
    into them
When tractors drive the pale beets toward the factory
I sleep very soundly there at the edge of the world
After
I made her greedy for ships and oceans

Angels

I saw one he came in a taxi the front seat
Was laid flat that way he had room
They lifted him out in front of the little fishmonger's
Escorted him into a shorn garden
There he stood serious in the air overtowered
Those who supported him nothing reached his eyes
His clothes were faded remnants of gold
Coated his chest he was without wings
His guides leaned him against a cart
Blocked the wheels before so he
Wouldn't begin to slide get smashed
I saw his hands they were empty
Probably carried the olive branch before or
Played a lyre for centuries
Now he was on his way in a taxi looking for an apartment
First to the antique shop what will become of him who
Really needs an angel who's that big
He fills a kitchen would stand
Where a refrigerator would make more sense or the table
With the bread-slicing machine, the solution
For him would be a kindergarten if it gave him shelter
Who wouldn't like to grow up with an angel

Reading Trees

The rain falls into the ground-water
It's the only use
It has in winter, unless
I related it to pines and firs
The dust of blossoms and paths
Is now being washed thoroughly
Off these northern trees. The trunks
File past me (I'm exaggerating:
I walk along the path) the trees are letters, I
Move as if on paper, jump over
The spaces between with effort, trip a sign down
This here is a coniferous forest
No underbrush everything clear
From line to line, the ground full of snow
Which comes from the rain, white as paper
A strange group of trees
Obviously from abroad (they
Don't grow like that here) pushes in, I circle
Them with slow steps: six trees
The first one the biggest, it would make a good mast
Towers into the invisible sky, up high
A wisp of fog, the smoke of a steamer
The trees lie moored, the hand
Of their ship's clock jerks to the full hour
A crash I'm not afraid, yes
Those are shots! now we move forward
A challenge upward, down
With stupidity exploitation hunger my word
Shines red
A forest with me! Mayakovsky
Blows the flute to his spine
I read: Aurora

Winter

I get to know myself, at present
The apartment which
Saw at least three generations
Of people the windows always
Had an arch at the top, the sills narrow
Barely suited for foliage in pots
The walls
Like trees' annual rings
Carry layers of wallpaper
At the bottom Art Nouveau, in between
Lining paper newspaper reports
Indignant readers on houses of ill repute
Two lines Reichstag fire then
Nothing but wall paper, the craftsmanship
Deteriorated. Or the view
Of roofs (barely a bit of sky) this
Is what they saw before me, presumably
Similar rain and snow, blackened
The asphalt in the court turned the walls red
Others
Shall see it too, a cat
Accompanies me a few years what
Does she know about me she loves my perfume
Or simply the place on which
I sit here I am not very good, but
Learned patience when I was small with
Watercolours:
If you don't wait, you lose the picture –
And sometimes
My heart moves on its sinewy strings
That is when I see a strange area

Hear of courageous people or
Someone asks a question;
I love my peasant coat my boots
And my sad face

I Wanted to Kill My King

I wanted to kill my king
And be free again. The bracelet
He gave me, that one lovely name
I took it off and threw the words
I had made away: comparisons
For his eyes his voice his tongue
I assembled the bottles I'd emptied
Filled them with explosives – it would
Chase him away forever. To complete
The rebellion I
Locked the door, sought
Out company, fraternized
In various houses – but
My freedom refused to grow large
This thing soul this bourgeois piece
Not only lingered, it became milder
Danced when I ran head-
First into walls. I followed
Up rumours in the country that
Spoke against him, collected
Three volumes of misdemeanours a folder
Of injustices, I even
Entered lies. At the very end
I simply wanted to betray him
I looked for him to complete the plan
Kissed the other one so that
Nothing would befall my king

Black Beans

Afternoons I pick a book up
Afternoons I put a book down
Afternoons it occurs to me there is war
Afternoons I forget each and every war
Afternoons I grind coffee
Afternoons I put the ground-up coffee
Together again backwards lovely
Black beans
Afternoons I get dressed undressed
First put on make-up then I wash myself
Sing am silent

May

On the roof of the big clinic
The sick on holidays will linger
In their striped and wide pyjamas
Put a finger on their sore spots
Smoke a cigarette in silence

On the earth the grass is emerald
Yellow flowers are mixed in
And the whitish kitchen women
Drag by carts heaped with potatoes
Meat compote and veg. Another

Ambulance is coming
With its flag and awful shrilling
Voice that shouts and screams for haste
Oh I see you pale as blossoms
Lying there beside your car

Elegy

I am the lovely bird Phoenix
Shake myself in the morning, say
I don't give a hoot! get it, my soul
White as a daisy
I am
The lovely bird Phoenix
But that
Won't make me fly again

Still a Light on in the Kremlin

This is Lenin's cat with white fur
Every night she goes patrolling
And her serious eyes of emerald
Peep on time out of the window

She eats wayward bits of writing
With her paw knocks down the inkwell
So that nothing can be read:
Masha slips through all the doorways

And if sentries stand before them
She will pinch her eyes so tight
Steering with her sickle tail
Safely through the pairs of black boots

When carillons ring the day in
Her goal is the library
She suppresses her sharp sneezes
Sits down on her favourite book

And recalls the times now over
Like the tracks her quiet paws made
When her master scolded softly
And began a clean new sheet

Moscow Day

Twelve on the dot the fountains behind Pushkin were
        ignited
I sat in the sun and smoked and the sparrows and pigeons
And other song birds that had just bathed
Were shot into the trees. Next to me a farmer in a black coat
Was seriously reading long stanzas. A grandmother walked
Across the square with a bundled infant. The bigger people
Strolled and talked and sat and read and were so at home it
        struck me:
I knew only myself and that was too little. Sat there
With myself on the bench me in the middle me to the right
        of myself
And to the left as well everything was free and taken so I
        decided
Not to speak to myself. I wasn't in any pain I didn't long
        for you I
Simply sat and the sun
Shone on me like on any other city meadow plane tree. All
        the fountains
Were visibly drunk they swayed in the wind like fountains.

Moscow Morning

Now morning dawns over the patriarchal ponds.
Anyushka spilled the oil there I a tear
The tomcat laughed considerably. I rushed
Up the sky on bent ladders
Close to the moon-body, oh the one who attracts me
Is not where I am. Does he live behind the windows
Flush with the ground? Margarita is coming Margarita
        is coming
Her legs flew past the window. Margarita warms
Margarita warms the stove with her clothes.
Once she's come she won't leave again. She'd
Rather be bad and do without Heaven than
Live pious and alone without the One. No
Matter what she does – now she is hanging
With her feather-adorned body on my bent ladder
Children's playground monkeybars by the ponds. We
Want to see you. You in the mandorla
Of my stared-out eyes I don't want to hang on to any finger
You can have them all, beneath me wags the tomcat
A German shepherd a Siberian lion the militia
So what do you think you're doing they ask me

Lithograph

The gate was bent and we got through
After paying a man with white hair
Who was not yet old and he gave
A bird-voiced Fräulein to us as guide

The old woman flew ahead, made way through stones
That seemed to us like the teeth of an animal
We imagined we were going into the mouth of the whale
That once was sent to swallow Jonah

They were stones in memory of old Jews
They died without violence in this city
And sank in layers into the earth, because space
Was scarce and surrounded by houses

Only large trees sprang up in this place
They stood leafless into the thin sky
Though they didn't seem to be low in sap

One of them grew from the rabbi's head
Until its roots had to leave him
Because nothing was left to feed the branches

The bird-Fräulein clattered with her beak
She quickly stuffed some dates into our ears
Before flying up to disappear among the branches

We run zig-zag through the black monuments
So that we are outside at present
This is not a place, we were on paper
Before, on stone, drawn and etched.

The Painter Ebert

And then we also went
To visit the painter Ebert on the edge of town
There we discovered: spring was: on the meadows by
    the river
Things already grew and the bushes
Beleafed themselves and birds
Trickled from them. Where he lives
The Saale softly bends and a little bridge
Spans the blackness with graceful arches.
In the wide stairwell the smell of old houses
Without waterclosets but you feel sheltered
Already we could see the pictures shimmer from white
    frames
Knocked then the woman next door said
He'd gone out and when he went out
Especially since his wife was at the hairdresser's he
Wouldn't return before nightfall. We asked
About his favourite bars
Looked into each one stuck our heads
Out of the sun into dusky taverns
Small smoky islands the bottles
Rang softly – one bartender
Had seen him go by suggested we
Try the next bartender down the road
But nowhere not in the Mohren not in the
Gosenschänke. And then the city began
We couldn't follow
Him any further the tree of taverns
Branched mightily

In a remote wood house between roses
When summer heat was relieved by rain
Came to me the image of a dream. First it was two words
Bound through a fraternal and or or?
A big picture grew from it. The paltry landscape
Seemed to lie right before my door and I saw
In the background maple trees, in the foreground

Playboy and Cowboy.

There stand they and could be brothers
Friends never: too deep what separates them, the abyss.
The one just dismounted from the horse's back
His shirt starched with sweat, his mouth
Very thin. The other drove here from a city
And is now leaning against the flank of his car. Quickly
Both men move with different horsepowers
Over the earth's cropped and shorn pelt.

They're wearing jeans and jackets one like the other
But those of the pretty man on the right
Are richly decorated. So the bib of his trousers
Edged by silver borders, directs the gaze
(Oh painter's artistry) to the body's middle.
Probably beneath the fabric the boy is
Studded with silver all over. The one from the mountains
Perhaps even suckled by the same woman
Has trouble not letting his clothes fall apart:
Where the knees show, the jeans'
Blue has become clouded, and his chest
Shot away the copper buttons long ago
While fishing for salmon, into a desolate canyon or
Into the ear of the horse he's grafted onto.
But because outer appearances
Don't yet make the man, what he thinks and does

Can't be read off the tip of his nose, the painter
Gave both boys a medallion:

The patron saint of the decorated one, blond and
    well-groomed
Forced into a corset, smiles and blows smoke-rings
The cowboy wears his more hidden
Only the shabbiness of his shirt lets this one show
She is brown, without silver clasps, older.
On her shoulder sits a wild bird.

But both men are shaking hands –
What is it that still connects the two?
What is work for one is leisure for the other!
So I hear myself asking in a dream: whether perhaps
The world of money has split them, lets them hate
And no longer trade
Horse against Ford; everyone everything as aeons ago
When they rested at the same breast? Shall I rebuke
    the painter?
Has he painted reality? America?

I Would Like to Hold a Candle to Droste

I would like to hold a candle to Droste
Look into old mirrors with her, name
Birds, we direct our glasses
On fields and elderbushes, walk
Gurgling over the moor, the peewit is courting
Oh, I would say, your Lewin –
Isn't that a horse snorting already?

The curl a little lighter – and we walk
The gravel path, I the late-born
Would have served up scandals – at the spinet
Which stands valuably in the hall
We play horseback songs for four hands or
The forbidden one by Villon
The moon rises – we are alone

The gardener shows us how to cast for fish
Until Lewin arrives in his carriage
Gives us newspaper flags as presents, shots of schnapps
We pour down our throats, read
Both of us love the fearless one, his eyes
Are like green shadow ponds, we now
Understand thoroughly the craft of fishing

Contemplation

What a perfect white-faced clown I am
In the beginning my nature was carefree and happy
But what I have seen pulled my mouth
In the direction of my feet

First I believed one thing then the other
Now I no longer cut my hair and listen
To your and my fingernails growing, little chicks
Losing their down.

                *

I say what I have seen strange enough
People misjudge it concerns serious things
How funny they say when I speak of a misfortune
When they should laugh they're frightened

Only sailors and chauffeurs nod when I speak
Those in blue jackets can instance everything
Have the coordinates in their heads and
What was drunk before and after and then
They are silent

Calling Formula

Phoebus red-crashing wall of cloud
Swim
Under his eyelid mingle
With my hair
Bind him so he doesn't know
Is it Monday is it Friday and
What century has he read
Ovid or seen him am I
His spoon his wife or
Just one of those cloud animals
Clear across the sky

Call of Lamentation

Woe my snow-white trotter
With the pit-coal eyes
The mane braided with pearls
The very soft nostrils
The lovely vast shadow
Bolted! Ran
Three evenings away could not be moved
To come home. Did not take the hay
Ate the chaff at random
I thought I would die I felt so cold

The Property

On Sundays the girls come with their children to the
    property
They bought cheap years ago. Still no money for
Fences or stronger doors; so they go and look and count
What has disappeared: the pump, the cups, the fuzzy
    blanket –
Oh, you can really tell when you're single and you
Can't use hammer or plane, and they can rarely
Convince friends to come here because there is nothing
To tempt them, the sand: it does invite the girls
To sunbathe without their bikinis, the tiny children
Constantly demand this or that from their mothers and are
    always
Romping in the way. The men know this and say:
Better to come during the week. – Ring the apartment bell
    at six,
Another hour, then it's possible. – So the girls find
    themselves
Pacing off their plot Sunday after Sunday, lovingly
    brushing against
The grass and pines; they count and measure and figure:
One thousand marks for the fence, who will put it up? The
    woodpeckers
Titmice and jays perhaps? And does the old woman
    approach between pines
Whom, her pension is small, one offers cold cuts and
    pudding?
Who, nice as you are, is put up: and now one has three
    wishes? They would live as though in a fairy tale with
    children
And lovers in dachas in the summer and with never a care.
But as it is the girls, in the evening when the sun

Has browned them a bit, must escape with their children
     and bags
Because it would be risky to spend the night here alone
Strangers could storm the unfenced fortress, boyfriends
Would never believe their beautiful women's innocence
     and don't forgive.
The children are tired and chirrup like birds. The women
Laugh.

Snow

He had me jump over puddles and trickles
Obeying his cheerful commands. Long offices
Framed the square, black black
The street, the river, it was warm. K. had
Lost his gloves, we walked and walked
Three times over the river. We smelled of smoke
Our hair rocked heavy and I fished
Cigarettes from my pocket. On a bridge
Again – no one around, just a truck
K. laughed and had to declare his love for me.
Behind the Prinzenpalais he had me wait
And when we met the Humboldt brothers
He said 'well' and showed the left one, who
Deported W. Weitling from F. back then. Under the raised
    train
Night was a double crease. I had never
Seen things so black, and I didn't see
That until the next morning either when snow
Rose like down in front of the window sill.
Over my shoulder I said in the direction
Where K. was: Bygodsnow.

Tilia Cordata

Slowly years later I go
From the being of dog into that of cat.
I don't want to talk about it, only this:
I wanted to record something for him
A poetic image: this was suddenly sweet
As honey to me: the linden trees
Began to bloom and I had seen
That trees resemble girls
Blonde ones, their strands reddish
Casually curled. The big girls
You look into their
Half-long curls from below. A trace
Of earrings, dangling, spheres
Buds closed up all the way in the midst
Of spreading blossoms selling themselves cheap – I just
        thought
Now I'm already seeing girls? But this
Didn't apply to me, I saw his eyes.

The Air Already Smells of Snow

The air already smells of snow, my lover
Wears his hair long, oh the winter, the winter which
Throws us close together stands at the door, comes
With the greyhound sled. It scatters
Frost-flowers on the window, the coals glow in the oven,
    and
You most lovely snow-white man lay your head in my lap
I say that is
The sled that will not stop again, snow falls
Into the centre of our hearts, it glows
On the pails of ashes in the courtyard darling whispers
    the blackbird

My Words Won't Obey Me

My words won't obey me
Barely do I hear them again my sky
Expands wants to reach yours
Soon it will shatter I'm already
Breathing small breaths my heartbeat
Has increased sevenfold emits incessant
And barely coded messages

Tail Wind

How he chases me, how his cry
Carries me forward twenty-five
Gales a second
The whole day long, in the evening, and into the night.
I come into the world I sing before him
Exultation and laughter: the fingers
Of heaven's child on my shoulder.
And if I hear the voice of the One
Of great beauty
The headwind turns, I fly
And always towards him
Beatingheart how the house sways

The Merops Bird

The great
Very beautiful Merops bird
Flies off in spring when the first leaf barely shows
Flies to the south where shadows
Fall most vertically the stone
As warm as my glances at him

So I learned: great he is strong beautiful as a
Human being and if you know of him
The longing never ends. He flies yet he looks
Back flying, he moves off, approaching nonetheless.
Through the eyes. The blood. To the heart. O beautiful
    tale! A
Jumping from rock to rock; hope
Where space and time lie
Down between us. And does he come back? He comes.
Longed for wished back expected expected
So he looks back flying, not at me.
He approaches he moves off.

In June

God be with us! The pastor
Looked like Rübezahl and drove like the Devil.
Passed the most elegant cars by
Hanging onto the bumpers and wildly jumping over.
I thought I'd reach the city white-haired when the
Area began to look charming; avenues
Of linden trees chestnuts, one and the other pond
Showed themselves off; the blue high road
Became a hunchbacked skipping little snake.
I was in such a carefree mood. I greeted a pretty
Two-coloured horse on the meadow, my child
Counted nearly five hundred trees. The pastor
Said what it means to believe, that's how we drove
Down to the island where Caspar David
Once climbed into the chalk. In green
Then blue colour the sea now lay
With shells and a shivering starfish at our feet.
I sat on a milestone and saw
The dark sun gliding away, you
On the other side of the world. I slept
And froze the whole night. The pastor from Dranske
Read about Jacob and Rachel in the Scriptures.

The Forest

Power saws howl.
Where shade was, sky.
Day- and night-stars. The fond mosses
Melic-grass opium-poppy and thyme
Ask but why
Always just my foot?

The Window

Those many skies over
Very flat land! In the first
The magpies fly, in the second

Overbearing clouds. The third
For larks. In the fourth
I saw an aeroplane stand.

From the fifth the star twinkled.
Dead butterflies on the floorboards.
Before it collapses, a house is sold.

Alone

The old women in front of red houses
Red hydrangea crippled trees
Brought me tea. With dignity
They carried back the trays, took up
Listening and watching posts
Behind tittletattletwirl curtains

The Village

In the evening the stillness was perfect.
The crickets fell silent in their holes.
On the hill the oak
Stood black before a sky red as lacquer.

So I came to the village from the marsh.
Walked over the glittering stubble field
Star and stones shone brightly
In the houses the lights flamed on.

Ground-up dust on the road.
Knotgrass under my feet
Spread from door to door, a summer-day carpet.

Quietly Walls Cave In

Quietly walls cave in, the apple tree falls
Into the grass with red fruits.
On beaten-up bicycles children
Tear down the fields and the postwoman
Washes her hands of it all.

The Milvine

Thunder; the red flames
Make a lot of beauty. The coniferous trees
Fly along their whole bodies. A desolate bird
Spread out in the wind and still guileless
Sails high in the air. Does he have you
In his southerly eye, in his northerly me?
How we are torn, and whole
Only in the bird's head. *Why*
Am I your servant not then I could
Be with you. In this electric summer
No one thinks of himself and the sun
In a thousand mirrors is a horrible sight alone.

Market Day

I saw an olive grove.
He said that is an olive grove.
The twig on the back seat
To Nyons! Nyons! There a long
Turkish embroidered music hangs in the trees.
Your lovely gaze on the root of my nose
Or my knee. The shining
Faces of the fish. Olives
Olives, crayfish big as feet. Trucks
With woven chairs for country woman and country child.
The bell in its cage is already dancing and booms.
Many lilies fling open their cups, more serious flowers
Totter lose their heads. *Sleep a little longer*
Madame, wrap yourself
In my travelling coat! Pearl curtains
Jangle behind vanished cats.

The South

If it were up to me, I'd sit all day
Leaning on my lazy bed, comparing
The sky and images in front of my eyes.
A country dog flutters over the road;
The old paper factories! The green pure water.
My arm in it, the other
Reaching over. Thirty-nine degrees at best the Sorgue.
Petrarch comes toward us down the path with Laura
On a donkey. Both over seventy and Laura
Was smoking cigars. The painter Klapper pulls from his
    shoebox
Twenty-five pictures he's begun. An ochre opencast mine
An alluvial system to catch pigments with – all that
Under Mont Vertoux one day in September, which
Has already lasted a year

Mirrors

Empty mirrors in the house.
No one's lovely face. Clouds
Drift within it. The gentle the grey ones the ones
Eerily shattered by lightning. As though he were
In the war.

The Flood

Black mirrors doubled landscapes playing-card beauty
The cloud greets its twin, the sky a circle.
One trunk, two crowns each tree.

Your body am I, you smile at yourself.

November/December

Again he is taking
Walks on earth meridians, what kinda
Matchless northern lights does he see avalanches
Roll over his foot, white bears
Rock his tent. He knocks down
A cognac and sparkles me something, three days
Later he decides to return his body
Steams and is studded with crystals

In the Glass House of the Snow-King

In the glass house of the snow-king the birds speak sensibly. We are his guests, he doesn't look in until evening: he throws down wool blankets, a truckload of coal into the fire. We do what we want. He puts enough rabbit meat behind the wall, and we are many. When we want to sleep, he makes the birds fall silent. At night he walks around the house with a hundred wolves.

Bird of Prey

Bird of prey sweet is the air
I never circled like this above people and trees
I won't plunge through the sun like this again
And drag what I seized into the light
And fly away through the summer!

Post

Somewhere in the world my tree stands, for I know that every person is entitled to one tree. Also one species of grass and a particular bird. My bird, for example, can already eat seeds, settle on a tree, recognize an event. My bird's event in this wet-cold February should be pleasant, not a gigantic rain, more the arrival of a post van with letters from Laurel and Hardy, descriptions of life in the country, the border officials stick the decal of a protected species of bird or human being on the van and wave *Red Front*, outstretched thumbs show the direction the world is taking.

Fog

After summer was easy for me, after I drove from W. to G. on the Semmering train in October, a colour film with tunnel cuts, I walk around drowned in November. If I wanted to go shopping in the market hall, my tears would fall in the face of all abandoned things, the stuffed cashier ladies. My child, who at that time came home from school only to run into the fog with a rifle on his back, has nothing much to cheer about with me. At night I have phone conversations and rush around town. That isn't dangerous, at worst guards step out of the fog before the most important buildings and fade back into it. It falls down like milk, I see feeble light from windows lying far beyond the housing structures.

Waste

I walked across a square in Venice
Relieved, until it struck me
That there are stones here on which
Your foot stood in winter.
I saw the trees by the ocean
Mangy, and the pathetic park.
At night I drove into the canal
And scattered your lira into the water.

Crow Tree

Somewhere behind the high-rise – I live on the eighteenth floor – a large bare tree will stand during the day. At seven-thirty in the morning the leaves fly past my window, fall and rise in the current between the houses. They resemble the leaves of maples or those of the plane tree, but their wings stretch out further, the edges are curled up, the colour black. When the thermal power station has swallowed the first ones, it will still take an hour until the sky is empty. In the afternoon they fly back to the tree. Featherweight charred silk paper. A sheet of darkness is assembling, leaf edge to leaf edge.

Allerleirauh

But best of all: to walk with you
Or without you
Down the boulevards nothing in our luggage
But raisin bread, wine, and tobacco
To hold the people of other countries
In our eye for a moment and later
Talk about it, to describe the sky the snow
You come with the west wind and I
From the north, we carry
All of that together, the tiny horses
The vertical palm trees, the stars, coffee makers
In the afternoon half past four, when the bell
Swings and shouts in its cage

The Rest of the String

Kite flying. Game
For large plains without tree or water. In the open sky
Rises up
The paper star, unstoppable
Torn into the light, higher, gone for all eyes
And further, further

The rest of the string is ours, and that we knew you.

The Last of November

First to the exchange offices at the Zoo, the last
Little silver horses from all our coat pockets.
Exchange – a fantastic rate, there was some left over.
The wind the wind, uncanny child
Blew us in our beautiful cabriolet
To the Reichstag.
Snowberries trickled, small animals
Rustled in that horrible place.
This is the Wall. Patches of green limewash.
Little towers and look-out posts on this side and that.
Register everything, he says, the way Hemingway noted
The stinking horse during the retreat in Spain.
We drove and flew
Three times around the freshly gilded angel, met
Our dead poets in their cars (they flew
Faster and more beautiful than we)

Pandora's Box

At certain times, it could be the twelve Haydn nights, our men, whom we left in anger, have a certain power over us. They must never find this out. Possible happy constellations will be hidden from them because they would never dare hope for such a thing and because even after seven palpable years we have remained strangely alien to them. Writing here will go a step further. Make them feel safe on days when they can't get anywhere with us. They will always reach for the phone at the wrong time, and that causes us to be true to our last love again for years.

Billet of Thanks

This is a beautiful day. I sit down into it, the eucalyptus leaves fly down and up, up for a long time, and when I see the tree body naked and white I know what that is a lovely day. The Roman men strut proudly by, spit pretty streams of water into marble basins and the very sharp *Carabinieri* – why does the military still enter my mind – keep watch with feather hats and smoke; everything different from Prussia, even the time of day, and the moon lies athwart – oh how I thank my next to last country for catapulting me here.

Every Leaf

I'll tell you what I see sometimes
Every leaf singly on the tree or
On the gravel small sickles or how it will
Go on with me: short stop-overs
Pack it all up again and gone

In the Morning

He catches twocentimetrelong salamanders
In a drawer two by two metres
Sucha big guy sucha tiny thing, I'm doubled
Up with laughter; the dragon
Sinks his teeth firmly into my finger, small
Pain and because you're driving away

Pebbles

I get accustomed into happiness. The wagoner
Without coach and horse
Stands up to his neck in the river, gives
Cheerful commands.

Bears

Small sinking mountain ranges
Tap-tapped individual bears
Out of their dens under the Tioga Pass
They stood still in the serious air
Studded with crystals and really irked
The black the ice-bound lake
Endured our foot, many silent birds
Flew from beheaded firs, the low clouds
Were put in motion this way came apart snow
Falls onto your mouth the white flurry
Wants to lead you away from me, and now.
I love you come look I am
In the midst of bears I am speaking truly
And if these powerful animals
Run through my head like this
They must have stood there
Early December their paws in the wind

Downhill Run

We threw our fur coats, our caps
In the snow into the trunk of our car and reversed
The landscape in the blink of an eye. Creeks
Leapt at our side, the other sun
Wasted itself, many red flowers
Fluttered over plunging meadows and gates
Of copper mountains swung open.

Day Stars

On the assembly line of the highways on a plain
With palm-heads crane-houses and glass bars
The sun on its feet very early and always grand
We saw crows the size of eagles these horrible animals
Clotted the strange trees water cannons
Constantly shot colour at the mighty grass
The date the name of the reigning god
Appeared to us in the sky and stars and stripes

Country Lanes

We couldn't remember
In what spot the water
Went down underground and since when
We'd been following these electrical wires
The flowers must have dried up long ago
The mountains lay like grey donkeys
Five horizons away and we rolled
In the glittering colourful air
Onto an infinite earthen plate.

Metamorphosis

Down in the low streets, my heart
Flew into my head in the falling lift
It still clatters like mad, we now swing
Through people and cars, screaming leaflets
Offers from Heaven, from the Devil
End up in our reluctant hands
Bodies move like atoms, clot together
Separate again, fuse, a sluggish pap
Oozes in the shafts of dam-like walls
Pushes together, buckles, the tops
Of hulking houses sway in the smoke
Of plunging clouds. I don't feel myself.
Now everything goes dark. There is
No hold for the fluttering eyes
In this insane city, and tears
Fall from me to the ground; I puke head over heels
Relieved into the gutter. This filthy place
Remains motionless, no longer swims before my eyes
I hang over your arm, distinguish
Voices and tongues, I recognize people
Again, the beautiful, the rich ones, the grey ones
Who live out of garbage cans, the girls
Blue-feathered children, bearded Jews.

Nature Reserve

The cosmopolitan rabbits
Hop their fill on the Potsdam Square
Looking at these meadows how should I
Believe what my grandfather told me
This was the hub of the world
When he chauffeured a beautiful girl
In his Adler when he was young.
Through the vanished hotel
Black martins fly
Fogs rise
From magical meadows and bushes
No sooner do you keep humans out
Than nature does her part grows through
The very pavement the streetcar rails.

Realm of Earth

News from the life of caterpillars
. The cuckoo stutters and the baked beds
Tear apart when I haul my watering cans
Look helplessly at the plants placed in my care
Lice-ridden vegetables, when I went
Into my father's garden years ago
The seven-fold plagues didn't exist
No hellish vermin and the soil
Still did its bit, this one here
Is a drop-out malicious and lazy
You have to beg it blow
Dung up it front and back otherwise it won't produce
As much as a pea how must people have
Insulted the realm of earth, a scattered angel
Appears before me to rescue
Twenty-seven rose trees the yellow canister
Strapped over his mildewed wings
His heavenly thumb in a rubber glove
Lowers the valve and for hours
There's the smell of bitter almonds.

Spectacle

The magpies on the steep roof
Impossible to tell what they're aiming at
Toil for nothing nothing at all
Long-tailed shuffling striding
Constantly transformed tragic comic birds
That take a bow at the end the crows
Are pale in the face of such cunning such art

Going to Seed

My God they're ferns after all
Green peacocks and ostriches
That took a seat in the rose bed
Did they fly in a storm
Or did they simply leap
From sleeper to sleeper along the old embankment

In a Dream

The lost man knocked in vain
The crumbling doors could
Offer nothing human

The Sign

A mole the live
Warm food of teeming maggots
Leaves the earth in broad noon light
The farmer kills it and sees
His barn that evening
Ablaze with bright red flames.

Noah Nemo

Evenings he concludes the logbook, opens
The big Hölderlin edition while
The Nautilus slowly pushes its old-fashioned towers
Lonely terraces overgrown with eelgrass
Slowly into the moonlight. It's
Pointless to wait for the directive.

Different Time

In the morning the fog grazes
On deserted meadows
The voice of the bantam rooster
Sits between door and hinge.

The pretty roofs crouched houses
Approached in the cold
Unfamiliar things surface from
Black gardens stripped of leaves.

In the pale vault of the sky
The old writing of bird migration
Grows up plateland's rick mountains
Plastic sheets court snow.

Oaks and Roses

I bought myself a timetable in Ferlinghetti's
Shop and I'm sitting in a Pullman coach
Riding along the coast day and night and the poet
Mirrors his cow skull in the window we drive
Forever into Wyoming line for line man
Oh man that's some speed and I see him with a
Karakul fur hat in a sheet metal village the swaying
Telegraph poles are about to fall over and the cruising
Limos howl like wolves, on a crossing.
The world is a farmstead in winter we can't
Get in flying fog when I go to the window
And the glorious trees in Germany
Wander incandescently by as American oaks
In the Presbyterian churchyards roses rot
And his poem keeps on banging rail joints
Wicked wicked abstruse crows are speaking
And when it's gone extremely dark and we find ourselves
Conspicuously well and the steppe in our gaze white heath
On the Trans-Cyrillic train, come
Into the open friend and spelling live backwards
We ask ourselves what could have become
Of the wild boys Yevgeni Andrei in the meantime
    and we fly
Through the infinite unbuggable birch forests of the Czar
Lev Kopelev waves to us a platelayer
With a sack of black native soil his huge head
His white beard accompany us a long time simply can't
Be wiped off the window before the pretty coach
Ascends in autumnal flaming flames.

Cold

Muted barking of dogs lantern-carrying
Children on St Martin's Day when the Saint
Rides through the village and over the fields.
The cracked bowl of the sky
The trail of insignificant minor stars
Such long unreciprocated love of assumed
God kills the heart in the masonry of night.

Motionless

Day arrives from the forests
Invisible it's snowing into the borders
Of tomorrow and today I can
Distinguish nothing on the earth
Everything is indistinguishable and equal
The tracks of wolves of lambs
The frozen hares are blanketed by snow
It lays itself on blown-over trees
The living ones it wants to suffocate
It lets brooks disappear
Moors and ponds fields everything is
Equally dead and buried in the twilight
Sinking twisting snow the eyes
Become confused black flakes
Ashes don't fall rise up or the sky
Is lowering itself because creatures are crouching
Breathless motionless the silence insubstantial moonless
It isn't light and won't grow dark
No one walks on the fields the fields
Fields of the dead grow shepherdless by the hour
The snowfall lasts long as my life
I have forgotten the name of the town
And the streets abolished squares
We are located shortly after the peace
We can't remember what
Happened the extinguished consciousness
Deserted without thought no light
No shadow dotted images and only
The strength not to move.

Woodland Piece

The north wind dismembers clouds
They ride across the sky up to the
Wolfish tundras the sun rises
What it brings to light barricaded
Forests demolished huts in the thicket
The tears of demonstrators no grass
Grows over it concrete settles.

Mental Arithmetic

White fog has made way for grey
The remote farms the glowing
Dung heaps few colourful roosters
Can do nothing against this sadness
It smells of tideland of bro-
Ken dikes winter tragedies
Names of the missing years later
The coat button turns up fog
Channels destitution into low houses
The calves beshit themselves and the milk
Becomes flocculent grey ulcers
The fields lie the mangy
Meadows full to the rim with disaster black
Smoking brooks without motion.
An incomparable exhaustion
Let curses and sighs go mute silence
Thunders in your ears with mole faces
Old men sit behind falling
Heavy drapes count the graves.

Heathland

The sun blinded me I walked
On Irish heathland
Snipes hurried clattering wings
Brought on a throbbing heart
Birches hit me roughly on the back
From far away I heard
Axes plunging trees
A newspaper I could not read
Drifted with the wind, from the dunes
Figures with sparse hair emerged
Eyes like stars floating feet
The way they're described
In old books shot each other dead.

Twilight

It's dark green beneath the rain
The old vaults of oaks
Neck-deep the uncut grass
The low trailing clouds
Meet people who walk around
Dreamily in sunken villages
On the sea's floor and dogs float
Through a paradoxical existence
The black algae the drifting seaweed
Swimming birds flying fish
Cause a lot of apprehension
Above the roofs we see the keels
Of English warships pass.

Lives of Cats

But poets love cats
The uncontrollable gentle
Free ones who pass the November rains
On silk armchairs or on rags
Sleeping dreaming silently
Give an answer shake themselves and
Live on behind the hunter's fence
When the obsessed neighbours
Still note down licence plates
And the man under surveillance in his home
Left the borders behind long ago.

Condemnation

Because he was not permitted to die
Chained to the native cliff his gaze
On the drifting clouds and always
Alone the images in his head voiceless
From calling, imploring, cursing
Staying alive required no thought
Divine cunning fed him so he slowly
Became used to fate years later
He liked to see the eagle approach and spoke
To him in stutters while he did his business

Or with inflamed eyes contorted neck
Because the beat of wings was overdue the low woods
Foisted a reprieve on him for days
He awaited the only being and
In the emptiness of wind of blazing sun
Believed when the pinions' dark gave him one moment
Of refreshment that he was sheltered
Loved the torturer credited him with virtues

When the chains crumbled the god
Tired of thinking of him
The eagle continued to fly because no
Order arrived to stay him
He wasn't able to rise to
Leave this terrible place forever
For all eternity he watches at noon
For the one who shadowed him.

The Fiery Furnace

The dead rise in autumn from the
Streams and rivers compliant winds
Show moving pictures on the sky the outcome
Of murderous battles flung down
Corpses souls frozen to death corseted
Throats bodies held by grey rags
Float above the bent labouring people
Before they are blown away the sun
In the mirror of the sky lets
Desolate pathetic clouds
Rise and wander again.

Demetrius

Like an oriole I live
In the crowns of trees
Don't touch the ground
Love the clouds but the
False emperor whimpers
He wants my soul.

His speech was rigged now
He's reached the end but I
Live in the tree
Crowns for ever
Laugh about the
False Dimitri the whining
Wood without a blossoming bough.

Freya's Cats

Over the ocean the evening star
Rises now and Bjarni claims
It's the goddess of love:
Wrapped in a glow and merciless
She smiles from the chariot
Pulled by white
Purring cats.

These lovely animals. Licked clean
What they hunt now are men.
These sky animals are fitted
With girls' eyes and bring
Joy and all suffering thereafter.
The scratches says Bjarni they deal
Remain forever.

Under Way

My body which accompanies me
Pursues me all my life
Formed by a dark
Shadow like a dog wild about
Being around me

A few words written in
Chalk on the street in the
Rain

Snow Warmth

That winter I lived
Caught in pack ice.
God's lioness the sun
Burnt behind the earth star.

In the twilight I found
Dead souls the shadows
Of frozen lakes and rivers
Blank without life.

A pelt had grown.
The ice between my claws
Drew blood I saw
Where I came from.

For a long time I heard voices
Always it was the same
Inexplicable cutting wind.
I felt happy in the pack.

We went to villages killed
The first whimpering lambs
From the rim of the sky
Winged animals broke loose.

Then I grew heavier carried
A litter of untamable children
When the fork-shaped beings
Handled fire and flame
You had to beware.

Winter Music

Was once a red vixen
With high leaps I went
To get what I wanted.

Grey I am now grey rain.
I got up to Greenland
In my heart.

On the coast gleams a stone
On which is written: no one returns.
That stone is shortening my life.

The four ends of the earth
Are full of woe. Love
Is like the snap of the spine.

April

Like clusters of lilac the
Blue crows now sit in the bushes
Sluggish feathered animals when patience
Draws its thread through the old
Carpet of the meadow again the popular
Pattern of last year develops. As long as
Life is its own mirror
Image we won't be frightened.

Sparks

Restlessly roaming I came
To this place and that one always
Found water intoxicating berries
A faded coat thin
As the ears of a cat.
Rhymes and lies I told
Those who yearned for them
It grew back like
Lizard tails and
Snake skin sparks
Leapt from the glowing
Coals until my time here passed.

Crow Chatter

My guiding star is a fist-
Sized planet and my compass
Lies on the bottom of the sea
But hope wants to dance
Only the sparrow hawk above the plain
Reads our thoughts.

Earth and people have
Run wild completely no
Reasoning will help the block
Is under way in free fall
And I myself
Stem from a family of wolves.

Recent Poetry from Anvil

BEI DAO
Forms of Distance
Translated by David Hinton

CAROL ANN DUFFY
Mean Time
FORWARD POETRY PRIZE
WHITBREAD POETRY AWARD

HANS FAVEREY
Against the Forgetting
Translated by Francis R. Jones

HARRY GUEST
Coming to Terms

JAMES HARPUR
A Vision of Comets

FRIEDRICH HÖLDERLIN
Poems & Fragments
Translated by Michael Hamburger

MARIUS KOCIEJOWSKI
Doctor Honoris Causa

CHARLES MADGE
Of Love, Time and Places
SELECTED POEMS

DENNIS O'DRISCOLL
Long Story Short

PHILIP SHERRARD
In the Sign of the Rainbow
SELECTED POEMS 1940–1989

SUE STEWART
Inventing the Fishes

A catalogue of our publications is available on request